PRAISE FOR TRISTA MATEER

"*Aphrodite Made Me Do It* is a gentle scream from outside of your window. It is a reminder that it's okay to let the light come in, but only when you are ready. You will find grace between these pages and a little sadness, too - the kind that makes flowers grow in all of the places you need them most."
— Wilder, author of *Nocturnal*

"*Aphrodite Made Me Do It* is a dazzling portal of a collection. Trista Mateer erupts with spells of thunder and then gifts you with a careful platter of language to cast them yourself."
— Blythe Baird, author of *If My Body Could Speak*

"Trista Mateer's work has the kind of sumptuous quality that leaves you breathless. *Aphrodite Made Me Do It* is an incredible offering from a truly valuable poetic voice that channels love as the ancient and powerful emotion that it is. Combined with the poet's own art, this book is a vibrant labyrinth, a treat for every reader. Mateer is magnificent as always."
— Nikita Gill, author of *Fierce Fairytales*

Winner - 2015 Goodreads Choice Awards — Poetry (*The Dogs I Have Kissed*)

"Gut truths and gin-clear imagery, Trista Mateer reminds us of all those places left unexplored by language." (*Honeybee*)
— *Foreword Reviews*

"This is a collection that will beg you to be dog-eared, coffee-stained, and shared." (*Honeybee*)
— Amanda Lovelace, author of *the princess saves herself in this one*

"Trista writes about love so honestly. It's messy, reckless hope. It's sticky-fingered stubbornness. This collection is a must-read for any queer femme, and for anyone who has ever lost themselves in a feverish want." (*Honeybee*)
— Clementine von Radics, author of *Mouthful of Forevers*

APHRODITE MADE ME DO IT

poems, prose, art

TRISTA MATEER

central avenue publishing

2019

Published by Central Avenue Publishing, an imprint of Central Avenue Marketing Ltd.
www.centralavenuepublishing.com

APHRODITE MADE ME DO IT

978-1-77168-174-2 (pbk)
978-1-77168-175-9 (epub)
978-1-77168-176-6 (mobi)

Published in Canada

Printed in United States of America

1. POETRY / Women Authors   2. POETRY / Subject & Themes - General

10 9 8 7

for you,
and the story you deserve

TRIGGERS

body image
sexual assault
rape
eating disorders
queerphobia
emotional abuse
physical abuse
gore
blood
death
fire

and possibly more

CONTENTS

APHRODITE
MADE
ME
DO
IT

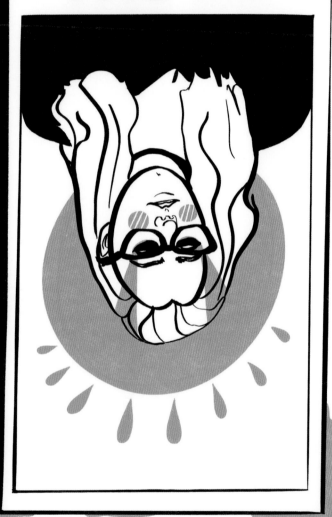

INTRODUCTION

I watched my mother lie for love
when it stomped through the house and
put its fists through our walls.
I watched her bleed for it and
lie more.

I told myself I'd never wear thin for it.
I'd never break for it.
And then I did.

I was human.
Small and predictable.

Bad love wanted a sacrifice,
so I made myself one.
I drank it straight from the tap,
wiped my mouth on my palms,
picked up a pen,
and called myself a poet.

The thing about embracing your own chaos
is that it never becomes clear
when you need to
stop.

I didn't forget how to fight for myself.
I forgot that I could.

THE DREAM GOES LIKE THIS

I'm on the verge of sleep, and then I'm not. I'm standing in a concrete room and my whole body feels like it's vibrating. A neon sign blinks on somewhere behind me with that distinctive sort of plinking and buzzing. The sign stretches nearly floor to ceiling with glowing, white letters that spell out the words: WHAT DO YOU NEED? WHAT ARE YOU LOOKING FOR? It looks like an art installation at a gallery somewhere, like there should be sculptures and people milling about. Instead, there's only me and the buzzing and the vibrating and water at the center of everything.

Square and constructed of individual stones instead of concrete like everything else, a well sits in the middle of the room. When I walk over and gaze into it, it's like I'm looking down at the ocean from the window of a plane. Everything is teal and coral and gold. Then I see the scallop shell and the figure towering out of it. She rises out of the sea, into the sky, closer and closer until I back away and she crawls out of the well like some horrifying truth. She sits on the edge of the well with her feet hanging down toward the water she came from, and she looks at me curiously. Her whole body burns with light. She says, "What do you need? What are you looking for?"

I understand who she's supposed to be. I just don't think I need anything she has to offer. I say, "I'm sorry. I'm not looking for love. I must be in the wrong place."

When she laughs,
the sound of it
swallows
my whole world.

3 of SWORDS

APHRODITE AIRS HER GRIEVANCES

I was worshipped on the battlefield once.
They brought me blood
before they brought me perfume.
They started wars in my name.

After a little time, men did what they always do. They didn't try to understand, they tried to explain.

They made me earthly. They branded me woman. Then they saw things in me that didn't mesh well with woman. They saw parts of me they didn't understand and they broke them off. They called me a hundred different names, an epithet for everything. Couldn't even bother trying to comprehend it all together—that I could be bloody and beautiful, that I could be divine and approachable. Men wrote the stories of my birth as if they were standing on the shore when I was spat up onto it. They picked up their pens and waxed poetic and nobody questioned it. Nobody asked me instead.

I am older than the poets
and I am older than the pens.

I am older than the stars
and the ocean I crawled out of.

They called me Gravedigger. Shining Queen of the Underworld. Aphrodite the Unholy. I had glorious names before they called me anything sweet. Before they started calling me smile-loving, shapely Aphrodite. They took my name and dragged it through the mud kindly. They catcalled me until people couldn't separate my name from sex. They made me a goddess of love and then vilified me for loving freely, for kissing and fucking and strolling boldly down the streets of Cyprus. They married me off in the stories so they could call me Adulteress, but I brought the god of war to his knees.

I belong to no one. They never wrote that part down.

The church
turned me into
a symbol of lust.
Called the apples
in my cheeks
sinful.
Said
heaven
would spit
my body back out
because it had
no place there.

I never needed
anyone else
to make a place
for me.

I have run naked
through Eden.

I have chased
the universe
to its end.

They whittled me down
one piece at a time.

They took my anger.
They took my voice.
They took my story.

They colored me pink and wrapped me in floral. They scrubbed the dirt from under my nails. They wanted you to believe that love is weak, that you cannot curse and kiss with the same mouth. They wanted you to believe that the root of love is romance, soft and wide-eyed. See what they did to my stories? My temples? My statues? Regardless of whether you desire it, love is what sits at the core of the world. It is stronger than greed and hate and jealousy and pain. What brings us together will always be more powerful than what keeps us apart.

I am deathless.
I will have no eulogy.
I will have no mourners.
Mine is the mouth
that fueled creation.
Mine is the hand
that wields the blade
and I will never let you
forget it again.

ACE of WANDS

THE POET AIRS HER GRIEVANCES

I knew love could draw blood
and I still never went into it
with bandages in mind.

I went into it with ink.

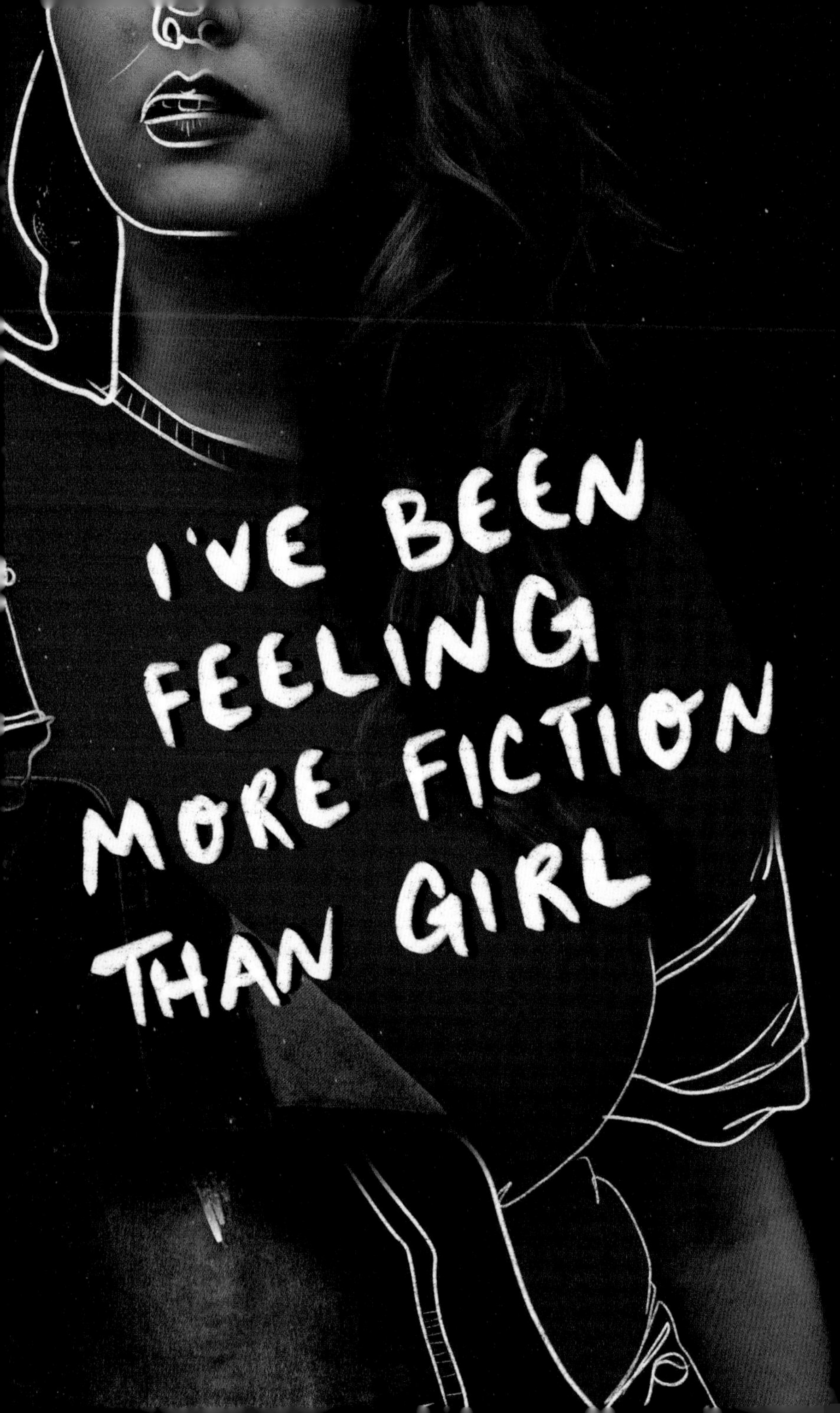
I'VE BEEN
FEELING
MORE FICTION
THAN GIRL

I wrote my own story
and still said all the wrong things.

I'm afraid to ask for what I need. I'm afraid of my survival seeming selfish. I'm afraid of my mental illnesses. I'm afraid of my sadness. I'm afraid of my anger. I'm afraid of the things that I want. I'm afraid of what people will think of the things that I want. I'm afraid of what people think. I'm afraid of my voice. I'm afraid of saying the wrong thing. I'm afraid of saying the right thing. I'm afraid of not knowing what the right thing is. I'm afraid of taking up space. I'm afraid of public transit. I'm afraid of the dark. I'm afraid of what men have done to me in the dark. I'm afraid of cisgender white men. I'm afraid of saying not all men and then having my face held down in the dirt by another man. I'm afraid of sex. I'm afraid of never getting over my trauma. I'm afraid of putting things down. I'm afraid of letting things go. I'm afraid of the emotional abuse I knowingly allowed myself to endure. I'm afraid of what I will let myself go through for love. I'm afraid of global warming. I'm afraid of being queer in public. I'm afraid of kissing someone in front of my mother. I'm afraid of not unlearning the bad things my parents taught me. I'm afraid of having children. I'm afraid of living alone. I'm afraid of checking my bank account. I'm afraid of wearing shorts in public. I'm afraid of driving. I'm afraid of driving and wanting to crash on purpose. I'm afraid of going to the doctor. I'm afraid of a doctor telling me to lose weight instead of listening to my concerns. I'm afraid of chest pains. I'm afraid of panic attacks. I'm afraid of not having health insurance. I'm afraid of moving away from home. I'm afraid of staying at home. I'm afraid of never loving someone as much as I loved the last person who broke my heart. I'm afraid of never being understood. I'm afraid of being understood. I'm afraid of forgiving too easily. I'm afraid of losing touch with my brother. I'm afraid of love. I'm afraid of other things.

My soft body
was a crime
in my mother's house.

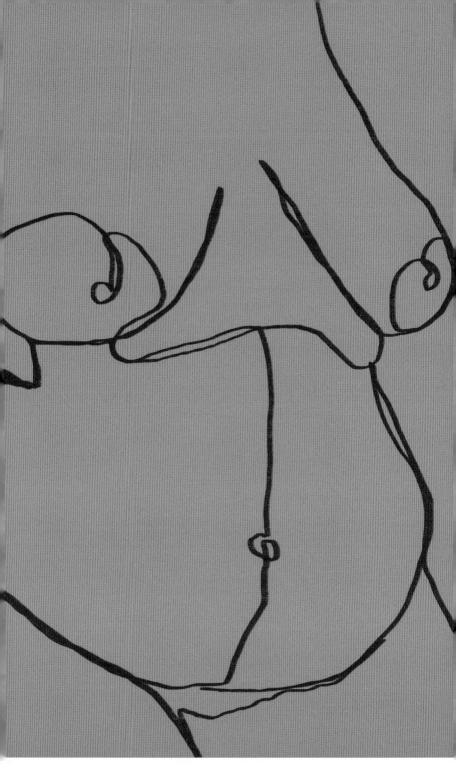

heaven
forbid
a girl
has a
body

I still don't know how to love a thing
even my mother is ashamed to look at,
but sometimes I grow out all my wild
just to sit alone with it in the dark.

When I say I'm not looking for love, what I mean is:

I don't like losing the part of myself that disappears when I date other people / I don't know how to let another person touch me anymore / I'm okay with my body when I'm the only one looking at it / I don't know enough about healing / I had to step back for a while to get to know myself again but now I don't know how to step forward / I worry it's safer to sleep alone / how can I possibly love someone right when I was raised with the worst examples?

STILL

I drew the tarot
cards. I made the rose
water. I sat out under the
moon. I put on my grandmother's
perfume. I crushed petals in the palm

of my hand. I split a pomegranate
in half and let the seeds spill onto
my dresser. I pressed some
to my tongue. And I sat the
rest out for her.

Aphrodite notes the romance novels piled by my bedside, their tattered covers and their dog-eared pages. She says, "I thought you weren't looking for love."

I say, "That doesn't mean I'm not hoping it will find me."

I say, "Isn't everyone looking for love?"

She pauses for a long moment before she says, plainly, "No."

QUEEN OF CUPS

APHRODITE SPEAKS ON LOVE

In the stories,
>   I cursed out of boredom.
>   I killed over jealousy.
>   I started wars for beauty.

In the stories,
        I was given agency
        only when my actions
        would make me seem
        spiteful and shallow.

They fabricated stories of my deeds
until people didn't know whether to
worship or fear me. They said I
was to blame for things that had
nothing to do with me.

I live with one version of history.
Everyone else lives with another.

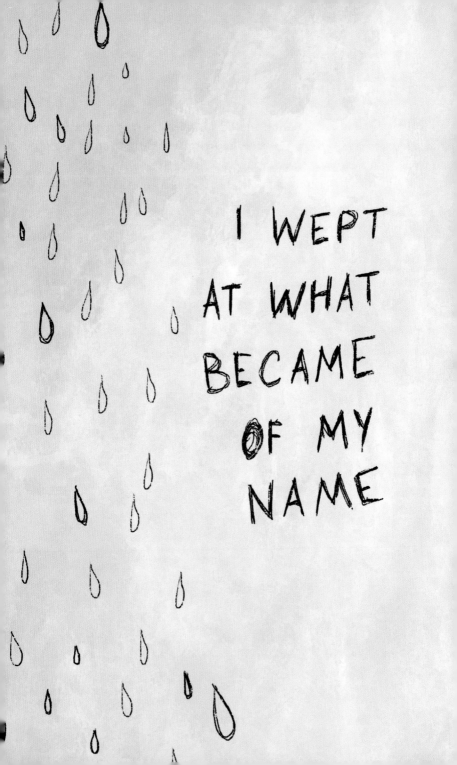

I WEPT
AT WHAT
BECAME
OF MY
NAME

No matter what the stories say, he was mine. Adonis, the one who chose me still, after seeing me for what I was. He was mine. Bled to death in my arms and he was mine. I felt grief for the first time and I taught the world to mourn with me. I taught them how to howl with pain. Just like I did. Like I still do. You'd think time would make me forget, but everything is written down. There is no forgetting.

It was my blood that made the roses red.
Did they tell you that?
My pain shaped the whole world.

Some people treat lost loves like stars, like guiding lights in the dark. You can spend your whole life following the past around if you really want to. My sister never did let a single thing go. It's true, she put Orion's body in the sky when he died. Now she sleeps under its light forever. It sounds romantic but her heart is so sore.

I treat my greatest loves
like seeds.

When I'm ready,
I put them down
and I seldom look back
at what has grown
behind me.

I keep my eyes
trained ahead.

There is always
more ground
to cover.

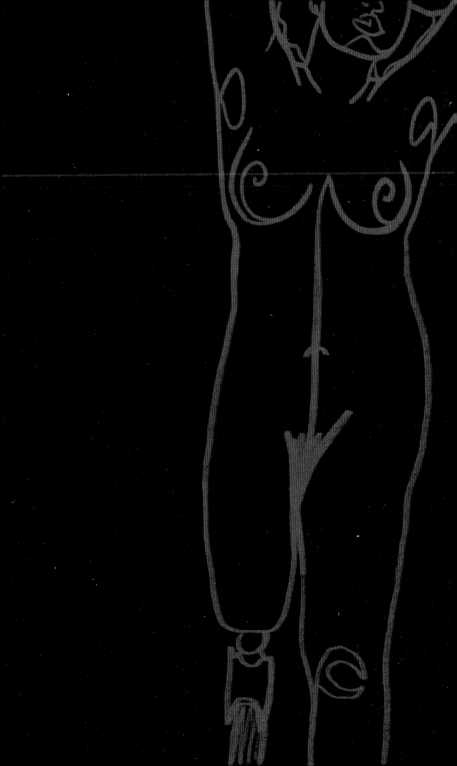

I spent
so much time
with Venus
that our stories
tangled
like legs
in bedsheets.
People forgot
the difference
between my life
and hers.

Things are just
like that
sometimes.

Love knows no face.
Love knows no gender.
Love knows no sexuality.
Love knows only love.

We waste so much time
trying to explain ourselves.

We thrive best
like gardens,
not singular plants
in lonely pots.

When people say you cannot love others until you love yourself, they fundamentally misunderstand love. Nothing thrives in isolation.

But you must
do the work
to make yourself ready
to love others
well.

No one else
can be responsible
for your healing.

MISCELLANEOUS THOUGHTS ON LOVE

love that doesn't last is still important / not everyone is meant to stay forever / love teaches lessons / love is more than the lessons it teaches / it does not have to be heavy / it does not have to be requited to be worthwhile / no one owes you their time or their affection / cherish your friends and the family you find with them / love has little to do with blood relations / and more to do with who you choose to bleed for / it's okay to walk away from things that don't feel right / your love will not always look like everyone else's / you will not always grow it the same way / you will not always express it the same way / people can love each other and still be bad for each other / people can love each other and still be incompatible / love never means you have to stay / it means your heart is open / fight to keep it that way

It is simple. You believe in the triumphs of love despite growing up in full view of its defeat because you are brave.

THE LOVERS

THE POET SPEAKS ON LOVE

I spent years

afraid to talk

about who I

had kissed

QUEER GIRL OVERTURE

I have this dream where I am not afraid to hold your hand in Texas. This dream where I don't have a visceral reaction to seeing gay pride flags. This dream where I can invite you home for Christmas dinner and my mother is so kind to you. And she asks where you went to school and she doesn't choke on your gender identity and she pulls me aside later to tell me how sweet you are. I have this dream where people on the internet stop changing the pronouns in my poetry. I have this dream where I know exactly what to say when my Southern Baptist relatives ask if I'm dating someone. I have this dream where I don't have to keep coming out over and over. Where people don't think my sexuality is a phase unless I can produce a girlfriend on command. Where people stop asking me who fucks better, men or women. Like those are the only options. Like the answer wouldn't be a gross generalization. I have this dream where people aren't always waiting to say, "maybe you haven't found the right guy." Where I don't imagine them jumping out from behind doors and bushes and shower curtains to say, "I hope you get over this in time to have children of your own." I have this dream where all of my queer representation isn't murdered on TV. I have this dream where my queer friends aren't murdered on the news. I have this dream where I feel safe. In rural Kansas. At my grandparents' house. In a gay bar. At Pride. I have this dream where I only write you love poems and none of them have to say, "I'm so glad we're alive."

My mother says:

are you still doing that gay thing? / can't you just pick one gender to kiss and stick with it? / if you have to like girls couldn't you at least like pretty, feminine ones? / why are you doing this to me? / maybe you should see a therapist

My mother says:

as the mother of a son, I hope people aren't listening to just one side of the story / yes okay I am also the mother of a daughter but that's not relevant / rape accusations can ruin men's careers / women lie about this kind of thing all the time / they lie / and they lie / and they lie

The night I was raped,
I walked right past my mother
and said nothing.
I was afraid to be
dusted for fingerprints.
I was afraid to be called a liar.

To stop resenting my mother I had to unlearn the idea that our parents are these infallible beings who always know the right thing to do, and do it. I had to realize that she's more than a mother. She's a person with unresolved trauma and she's scared of being alone and she's frustrated with existence, just like everyone else.

But this is how children are forced to bear the weight of their parents' traumas. This is how dysfunction breeds its way into family lines. You forgive your mother for the things she did wrong, because of the things that were done wrong to her. You expect your children to do the same. Everyone's backs ache under the weight.

Understanding
doesn't have to mean
granting forgiveness.

And forgiveness
doesn't have to be
a free pass.

MAKE
YOURSELF
A
PRIORITY

abridged list of things to let go if you want to be happy:

old versions of yourself / ideas about who and what you were supposed to be / other people's expectations of you / societal expectations of you / gender norms / heteronormativity / internalized ideas about what your life is supposed to look like / the idea that romantic love makes you whole / relationships that cause you more grief than they're worth / people who cross your boundaries / family that makes you feel unsafe or unwelcome / the need to make your happiness look like everyone else's

I'm trying to remember
to make room in my life
for the person I am now,

not just the people I have been.

Change is Normal

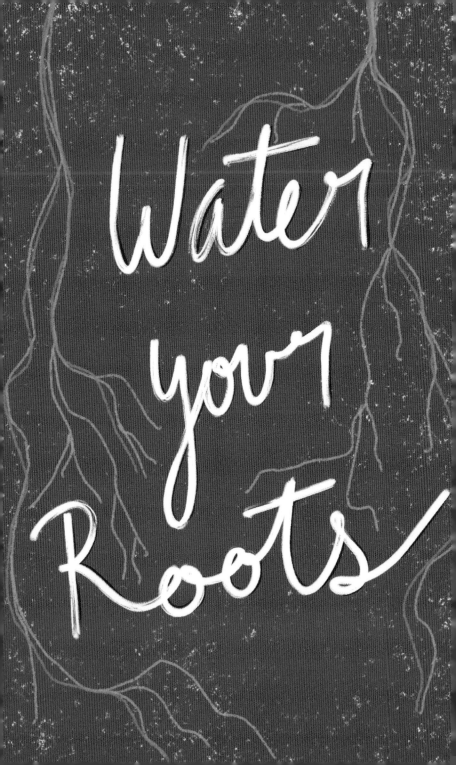

It's important not to isolate yourself when you're healing but it's also important to be able to sit quietly with yourself.

ALONE
DOES NOT
HAVE TO BE
LONELY

- make art
- plant trees
- read
- practice a skill
- teach yourself something
- learn to cook
- go for a drive
- make a new playlist
- sing
- meditate
- get organized
- travel solo
- go for a walk
- volunteer
- go stargazing
- take a long, hot bath
- declutter
- go to a museum
- garden
- write a poem

I'm still trying to figure out who I am alone so that I know who I am in front of other people. I will not be the girl who plays dress up. I will not be the girl who masquerades. I will not disappear into every relationship if I know ~~which pieces of myself are worth holding onto~~ that I am worth holding onto.

I THINK OF
YOU OFTEN

BUT I THINK
OF MYSELF
MORE

Aphrodite tells me that love is like wine. If your cup is already full and you try to add more, it will just spill onto the carpet. Some people try and try and just stain everything. Their fingers are purple with want. She says you shouldn't open a new bottle if you're still holding onto an old one. I tell her I don't drink anymore and she says to me, "You have to let something go. You carry too much in your heart. There's no room for anything else."

HOW TO LET GO

Materials:
- paper
- pen

Instructions:
1. Go somewhere quiet that you can sit peacefully. Breathe slowly. Center yourself.
2. Think of the person you need to let go of. Go over the relationship in your head. The good parts and the bad.
3. As you reach good parts of the relationship, thank them. Thank them for their space in your life, the kindness and the comfort, the happiness, the support. Thank them and release them.
4. As you reach bad parts of the relationship, consider them. Remember why you walked away. Remember your boundaries and your needs. Remind yourself why these moments are things you don't want to repeat. Send them away.
5. With the relationship fresh in your mind, write down what you still have to say. What is keeping you from moving on? Why do you still think about them? What would you say to them if you had the chance to be completely honest without repercussions? Write it down. Write until you have no more words left for this person.
6. Read the letter aloud to yourself. Give yourself the opportunity to speak your words. Put them in the air.
7. Dispose of the paper in a way that feels right to you, but that gets the thoughts and feelings you've written down moving away from you. The easiest method is sometimes to just go for a walk or a drive and to throw the letter away somewhere outside of your home. Trust the universe to carry it the rest of the way.

~~we never had room for~~
~~anyone else. Not in a real~~
~~way. I hope you're happy~~
~~and I hope you're okay~~
~~but I hope you never think~~
~~about me. I loved you deeply~~
~~but ... other people~~
~~deeper and ... more~~
~~reciprocal ...~~ Letting
you go is not letting
a part of myself go. It's
letting a part of myself
grow. ~~...~~

~~still important to me in it~~
~~... way that things can~~
~~be important but no longer~~

The same way
she rose from the sea,
you rise like a phoenix
from the ashes of things
that no longer serve you.

You mythic bird.
You unbelievable thing.

If love is a door I keep closed, will it be a wound I keep open?

I haven't learned
how to heal.
I've learned
how to be alone.
They're not
the same thing
anymore

but

romance
never gets to be
the biggest part
of my story
ever again.

STRENGTH

APHRODITE SINGS OF WAR

They vilified want but all of us are full of it.
Even me. Even still.

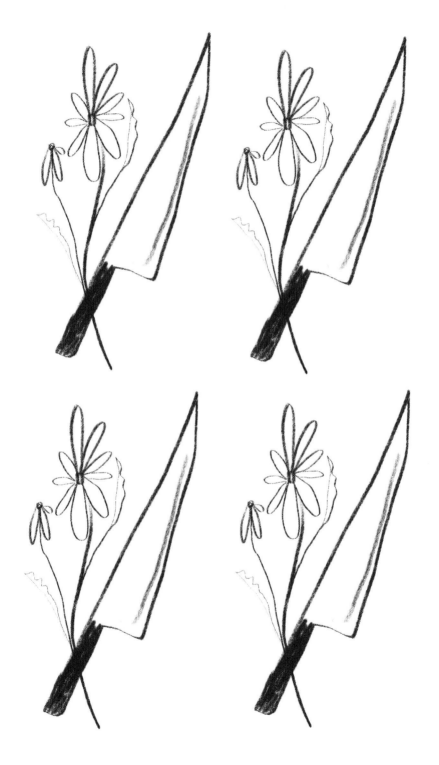

I stole the chariot of Ares
and rode it into battle. I
did not stay behind to
bandage wounds.
I raised armies.
I hefted spears.
They sang
of me in
Sparta
and
in

Troy.

To love something deeply
is to know
that you will go to great lengths
to protect it.

To sing of love
is almost always
to sing of war.

BATTLEFIELD

a blackout poem of Pat Benatar's "Love is a Battlefield"

young

hearts

demand

to

die

for   Love

In Troy
they fought
over Helen
like children
but Achilles
mourned Patroclus
the way a soul
mourns a body.

I have seen the best and the worst of the world and I have not let that break me. You will not let it break you either.

WELCOME REFUGEES
SÍ SE PUEDE
BLACK LIVES MATTER
PROTECT TRANS RIGHTS
the future is INCLUSIVE

I have played a hand in the crumbling of kingdoms and the humbling of great men. There are those who still spit my name. They call me The Deceiver. They call me treacherous.

When you fight for what is just, prepare to meet opposition. Remember, it is the good in us that stands in front of what needs protecting. There will always be reasons to back down but there will always be more to push forward.

The battles you fight
will not always be loud,
bloody affairs. Sometimes
they will happen in your
own home. Sometimes
they will happen in your
own head. Just remember:

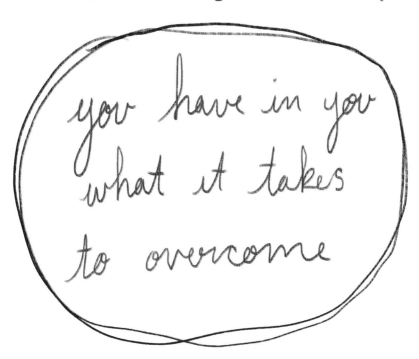

you have in you
what it takes
to overcome

You are not required to be small.
You are not required to be pleasant.
You are not required to be conventional.
You are not required to be accommodating.
You are not required to be submissive.
You are not required to be merciful.
You are not required to be quiet.

The stories sought to teach obedience,
as if every woman must be mistaken for Pandora.

Men said she was the perfect vessel for evil to enter the world, but men are the ones who wrote the stories. Men wrote the myths down and called them history, and time has dragged them further from the truth. Pandora's jar became a box. Eve's pomegranate, an apple. All the details change but one: it is a woman with her hand on the door to Hell.

No one ever talks about the loneliness that permeated Eden.

I know why Eve
stole the fruit.
I know why Pandora
opened the jar.

Can you really say you don't?

What would you give up to taste the universe? A rib? A bite? A garden? More, perhaps, but certainly not less.

When Pandora's story first met paper,
they did not even have the grace
to give her a name
before they blamed her
for every evil thing let loose in the world.

They said we molded Pandora from clay and dressed her in finery. They said we taught her to lie and to deceive before we handed her a jar of evils and sent her into the house of men. But I was in the room where everything happened. I watched Zeus gather the clouds himself. Pandora was made with precision and care. She was made of thunder and of rain. She was hard to look at, like all beautiful things, and hard to part with as well. Before she left, my sisters and I pulled her aside. Athena gave her the ability to create, Artemis gave her the gift of language, and I gave her curiosity and the desire to satiate it. I showed her the darkness in herself and told her she could have it if she wanted it, if she ever needed it.

And then she did.

She was not the first woman, but she was the first one I ever let leave with a piece of me.

They made a monster
of Medusa as well.
Hated how loud
her trauma was.
Couldn't believe
she had the audacity
not to take it lying down.
They made a war-ground
of her body
so she made one
of theirs.

Medusa wanted
to be untouchable.

They made sport
of her resistance.

Praised each other
for how close
they could get.

All of us are survivors until we are not anymore.

Athena and I wailed with grief on the day news came of Medusa's death. That man held her head up like a trophy and I wanted to smite him for it. I wanted his head for my own. I wanted to open up the earth and let it swallow everything. The world was full of men who called themselves heroes for crossing boundaries, claiming bodies like prizes. The world still is.

There is nothing inherently toxic about anger.
It is hard not to be angry.
There is no reason not to be angry.

Like everyone called a woman,
they say I had no childhood.
They say I rose from the sea fully formed,
forced to bear the weight of other people's desire.
It's not the truth, but it's close enough.

Not all gods are born.
Plenty of us rise.

THE BIRTH OF APHRODITE

When the world was young, I made a deal with a primordial force in the universe. It offered me something cruel and it was something I wanted. I'd never acknowledged it before. Had always tucked away the thought because that's how you live with bad thoughts. You pretend they only belong to other people. This thing unscrewed the jar of my darkness and poured it out on the floor between us. It said, you can have this. You can take this but it's going to change you.

Time is not linear. I see the beginning and the end of all things now. I know Pandora. I understand Eve. I have been them and I have made them, both. Their stories repeat, as does mine, in the hands of every person who scrambles to be both what they're expected to be and what they are. Everyone who upends their own darkness and swallows it.

I took my body to the water and this time when my tormentor came up behind me there was no cowering. No weeping. Only the blade pressed into my palm and the sweat on my brow. Parts of the old stories are true. I washed my hands clean in the ocean and I came out something else, different than before—but blood will do that to you more often than seawater will.

I feel no shame for my body. I feel no shame for my voice. I feel no shame for what I have left behind. I feel no shame for the love that did not fit. I feel no shame for my grief. I feel no shame for what I have outgrown. I feel no shame for who I have loved. I feel no shame for what I have loved. I feel no shame for the bodies in my bed. I feel no shame for discarding my old name. I feel no shame for disagreeing. I feel no shame for being loud. I feel no shame for taking up space. I feel no shame for fighting back. I feel no shame for my anger. I feel no shame for my defense. I feel no shame for the things I have done to ensure my peace of mind, my freedom, my space, and my survival.

DEATH

THE POET SINGS OF WAR

Once, someone asked me
why I write so much about airports
and I said: it's not about airports.

It's about having something
tangible to miss.

I don't know what to call homesickness
when I'm home.

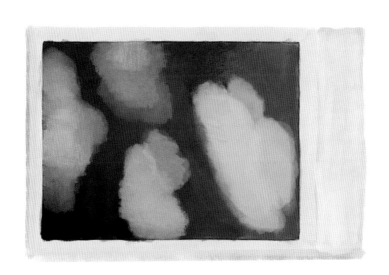

there's a
difference between
running away from
your problems and
giving yourself
the space to
figure things out

people always tell me
not to travel alone because of
men and the things they do
to women's bodies in the dark,
but I've met the mothers of
the people who assaulted and
abused me. I sat under the
bright, fluorescent lights of
their childhood kitchens.

all of them

& THEY HAVEN'T ALL BEEN MEN

People expect all stories of abuse
to be loud and angry
but they're not.

Sometimes they're quiet and cruel
and swept under the rug.

Your abuser's past does not absolve them of their abuse. Their depression does not absolve them of their abuse. Your relationship with them does not absolve them of their abuse. How long you've known them does not absolve them of their abuse. Your love for them does not absolve them of their abuse.

My pain is valid
even when people
make me feel
like it isn't

even when I
make myself feel
like it isn't.

I forgive myself for putting on my favorite sweater and thinking of you wearing it. I forgive myself for wanting to talk to you about that podcast we both love. I forgive myself for thinking about when our books used to be on the same shelf. I forgive myself for the poems I wrote about you. I forgive myself for still knowing your best friend's middle name and your favorite songs for long drives. I forgive myself for letting go of the bad things and leaving all of this behind.

I forgive myself for the years I kept your phone number afterwards. I forgive myself for wondering if I could retroactively consent. I forgive myself for thinking that if I could want you now, it would make what happened okay. I forgive myself for wondering if it was my fault. I forgive myself for staying so long. I forgive myself for the years it took me to say the word rape. I forgive myself for not telling the people we knew what you did to me. I forgive myself for my silence. I forgive myself for not being angry at you anymore but still being scared. I forgive myself for the mess of my trauma and the years I didn't know what healing looked like.

ON STILL HAVING THE OCCASIONAL TENDER THOUGHT TOWARD MY ABUSER

Even a match remembers
the moment before it was struck.

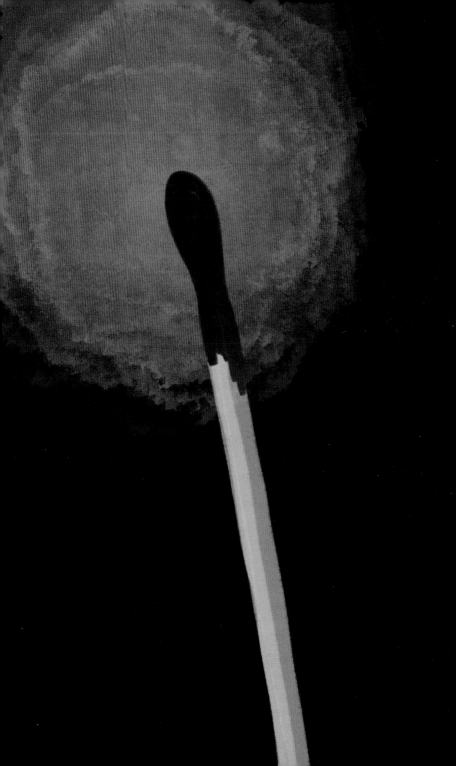

CAN MY ART
BE A HEALING
THING IF I
ONLY WRITE
ABOUT MY
TRAUMA &
NOT MY JOY

My pain has always deserved a voice and I will not deny it that, but I won't devote my life to it either.

Fuck another poem about everything that has hurt me. Fuck another poem that means I have to stand in front of strangers and make a bouquet of my trauma. Fuck another poem that prevents me from forgetting my abusers. Fuck another poem that adds weight instead of taking it away. Fuck another poem about my sadness. Fuck another poem about my emptiness.

Let me fill the space instead with joy.

I am surrounded
by love

As Aphrodite watches me scrub my bathtub,
she talks about the ugliness of practical architecture,
says we forget what beauty is sometimes
and why it's important.

She reads me her personal list of the most beautiful things,
and there are no people on it.

She says there's some dispute over the reason for our creation
but that it definitely wasn't to be gilded objects.
She says, *if you were only meant to be beautiful,*
we wouldn't have put you down here
in the dirt.

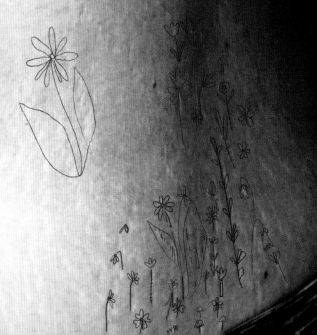

every scar is
evidence of
GROWTH

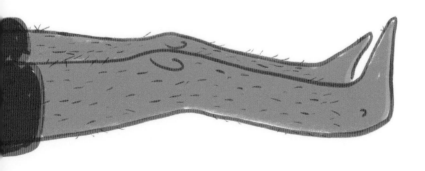

If my body
is going to
grow toward the light,
I need to let it
see the sun.

PERSONAL REFLECTIONS ON GENDER

I used to think girl meant wilting like a rose in the palm of a man's hand / but sometimes it just means thorn / and sometimes it just means wilting into my own hands / sometimes it means blue and elbow tattoos / lawn chairs and birch beer and lightly scented chapstick / sometimes it means being the knife / and the twisted ankle, bloodied lip / sometimes it means not being the poem or the poet / and choking on glitter / kissing someone else's hair / playing jump rope with the binary / and politely or impolitely deconstructing boxes / skin tingling at the thought of being called a pretty boy / or a star cluster / sucking the dirt out from under your own nails just to taste where you came from / without ever having to go back there

Accepting this body
did not mean convincing myself
that it was beautiful; it meant
giving myself permission
to exist regardless.

MODERN HYMN FOR APHRODITE

O' tongue-sharp blade.
O' bleeding heart.
She of many names given and taken.
Lady of the Unknown.
Lady of the Daybreak.
You bare-knuckled mother.
Righteous anger and holy grief.
You necessary rage.

Born not of the cruel sea
but of your own hand.
Self-made splendor.
Spark of creation.

The universe hums in your wake.
You leave nothing undisturbed.

O, you tender sword

MODERN HYMN FOR MYSELF

O' heavenly mess.
Parade of contradiction.
You long winter masquerading as spring.
You great thawing.
Saint of undeserved forgiveness,
of longing and of anguish.
You peach-bruised wonder.

In your name I will take my vitamins
and go to bed before dawn.
I will respond to my emails in a timely manner.
I will grab myself by the throat
but I will never let a man do it again.

NOW I SPEND MORE TIME LOOKING FORWARD THAN I EVER SPEND LOOKING BACK

3 of CUPS

RISING

Have I told you about Sappho?
Always overcome with longing.
Chasing honey and the bee.
Calling my name night after night.
Calling me down from the mountain.

Now she is remembered by the love
she kept trying to give everyone else.

You were not the first poet
to sing my praises.

If you have learned anything from me,
I hope it is to practice
singing your own.

FIND REASONS TO CELEBRATE YOURSELF

The past is no longer something
you have to drag around behind you.

You're made of the same stars as me.
You may not have walked fully formed
out of the ocean but
the past is the past for a reason.
Nothing that came before matters
unless you want it to.

DISTANCE
YOURSELF
FROM
EVERYTHING

THAT MAKES YOU
FEEL SMALL

It is never too late
to realize
you don't want to be
on the path
you're walking.
You can never go back
but you can always
chart a new course.

Chart a course toward bliss. Chart a course toward awe. Toward cheer. Toward enlightenment. Toward wonder. Toward fascination and tenderness and strength. Chart a course toward love. Build a life you're excited to live inside of and chart a course toward home.

give yourself permission to explore every aspect of your being:

the parts they call feminine and the parts they don't / the parts that would make your mother gasp / the parts that are deemed unacceptable and undesirable / the parts that are hungry / the parts that are angry / the parts that are hurting / the parts that make you feel good / the parts that make you feel guilty / the parts you're not proud of / all of it / every bloody, ugly bit

We use labels to help explain ourselves to others. They don't define us. We define them. If a word isn't working for you, make it work. Pick it up. Make it yours. Or put it all the way down and pick up other words. Make new ones. Language evolves and revolves around you.

you were
<u>not</u>
made to
be contained

You
do
not
exist
to
prove
anything
to
anyone.

you have always been enough

your healing
doesn't have
to be
pretty

No one can take your story from you if you know how to wield words. Their voices may be many but yours will be honest. You have the power to right wrongs and sing truths. You still have the pen in your hand no matter what you choose to do with it.

REMEMBER:

TAKE
RESPONSIBILITY
FOR YOUR
ACTIONS

RISK
THE
UNKNOWN

CHALLENGE
YOURSELF
TO GROW

learn
from
your
Mistakes

trust your gut

COMMUNICATE
HONESTLY & DIRECTLY

I stand in awe of your survival.

Let me leave you with this:
your life is short and
all the more precious for it.
I do not seek
to tell you how to live, only to live at all.

> to not fear the day.
> to know you are stronger
> than what has hurt you.
> to know that you
> will triumph.

MAY YOUR
LIFE BE
FILLED WITH
SO MUCH JOY
THAT YOU
WISH YOU COULD
SURVIVE IT

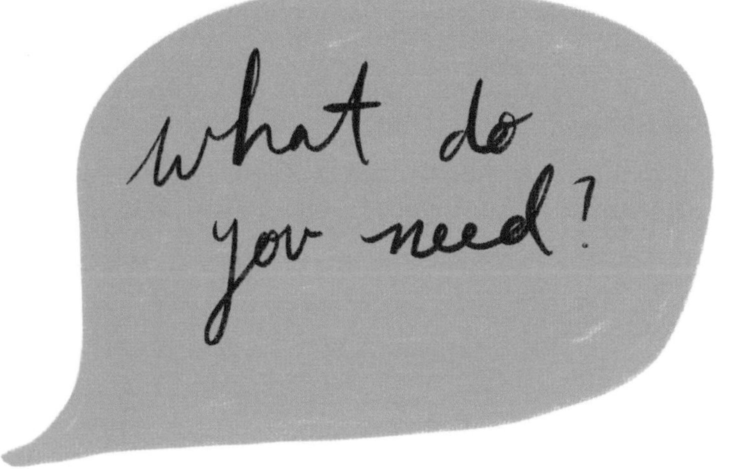
what do you need?

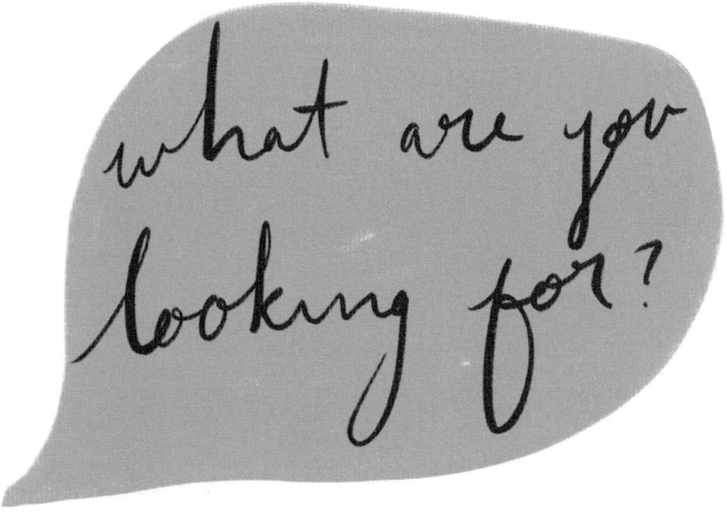
what are you looking for?

ACKNOWLEDGMENTS

Thank you to my poetry family: for the advice, for the love, for reading these poems before anyone else. Thank you to Mira Kennedy for the edits. Thank you to Lauren Zaknoun for the lovely cover work. Thank you to Michelle Halket and the team over at IPG for helping me send this book out into the world.

And thank you: for dog-earing pages, for highlighting your favorite lines, for sharing your stories with me, for sharing your time with me. Thank you for supporting me. Thank you for reading, always.

ADDITIONAL NOTES & CREDITS

"Queer Girl Overture" has previously appeared on *Thought Catalog*.

Some of the photos in this book, pre-artistic manipulation and editing, were sourced from a free-for-commercial-use website. Lisa Fotios, Zack Jarosz, Gabriela Pereira, Godisable Jacob, Min An, Kat Jayne, Daria Shevtsova, and Vinicius Costa are a few of the photographers I used. You can find more of their work on Pexels.

Trista Mateer is a passionate mental health advocate, utilizing her large online platform (and her work) to destigmatize and springboard conversations surrounding grief, loss, trauma, anxiety, depression, etc. A multi-faceted creative force, Mateer is best known for *Aphrodite Made Me Do It*—a collection of art and poetry—which explores modern feminist issues through the lens of Greek mythology. Whatever she's writing about, Mateer invites readers into a world where vulnerability is celebrated.

@tristamateer

tristamateer.com

THE MYTH & MAGICK COLLECTION